Norris and the Bath day

By
Catherine Richardson

Dedication

To my children, George, Noah and Milly, who are my life, and have been my inspiration since day one!

Acknowledgement

Dad, I wouldn't be who I am without you, unfortunately dementia has stolen you from us.I wish you could have been present to see this and be proud.

About the Author

Kate Richardson born in Ipswich suffolk,now resides in Oxford and work as a Biomedical scientist for the NHS.

Norris was a potato sprite

A green and jolly fellow

He lived in an old potato sack

With rotten spuds that were brown, green and yellow.

Norris had a friend he loved

They talked and played together

He was a lawn elf short and stout

A comely little fella

The only problem in the way

That made poor Norris mad

Was Eric's smelly odour

Which was very, very bad

So Norris tried to tell his friend

About his awful hum

He pondered hard for quite some time

And felt so very glum

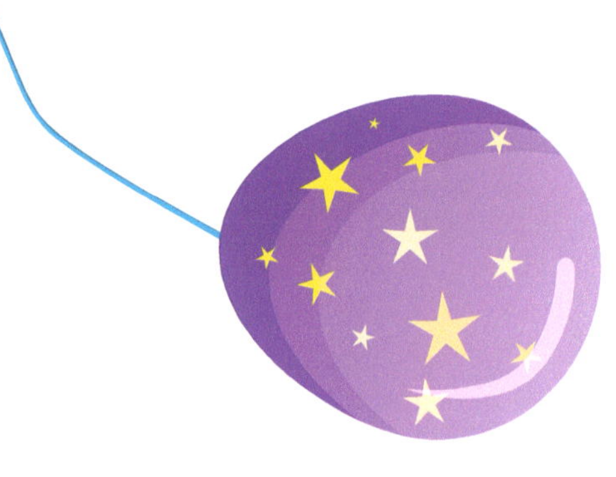

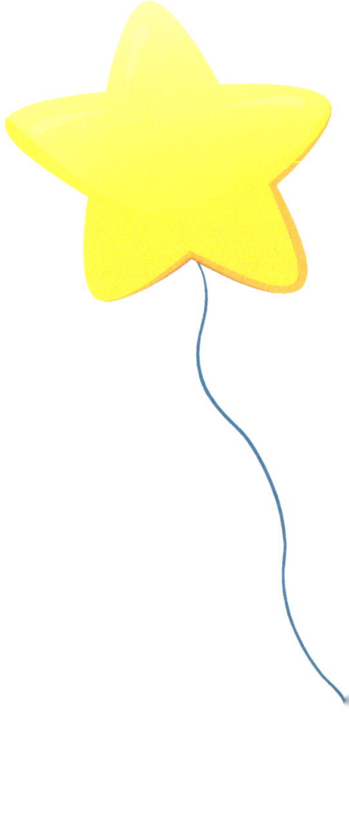

A bathing party was his plan

And thrilled him to the core

With thoughts of bubbly bubble bath

And scented soap galore

S S SOAP

A date was set and things arranged

To make the day just right

With party games and finger foods

Balloons so big and bright

Sun and clear skies did abound

As the day for the party arrived

Eric' face was a picture of joy

And Norris was very glad

HAPPY
BATHDAY

At first Eric was a little afraid

As washing wasn't his thing

But once he was in the bubbly bath

The fun could really begin

S
S
SOAP

So, if you are an elf so grubby

And all your friends think you stink

Don't be afraid of taking the plunge

In the bath or indeed the sink